COMMUNITY SCHOOL
Discovery Center

THE COMMUNITY SCHOOL
St. Louis, Mo.

## Let's Discover Canada

# NEW BRUNSWICK

**by**
**Suzanne LeVert**

**George Sheppard**
**McMaster University**
*General Editor*

**CHELSEA HOUSE PUBLISHERS**

New York                    Philadelphia

*Cover:* Drury Cove, near the city of Saint John.
*Opposite:* The day's catch is unloaded in Caraquet.

**Chelsea House Publishers**
EDITOR-IN-CHIEF: Remmel Nunn
MANAGING EDITOR: Karyn Gullen Browne
COPY CHIEF: Juliann Barbato
PICTURE EDITOR: Adrian G. Allen
ART DIRECTOR: Maria Epes
DEPUTY COPY CHIEF: Mark Rifkin
ASSISTANT ART DIRECTOR: Noreen Romano
MANUFACTURING MANAGER: Gerald Levine
SYSTEMS MANAGER: Lindsey Ottman
PRODUCTION MANAGER: Joseph Romano
PRODUCTION COORDINATOR: Marie Claire Cebrián

**Let's Discover Canada**
SENIOR EDITOR: Rebecca Stefoff

**Staff for NEW BRUNSWICK**
COPY EDITOR: Benson D. Simmonds
EDITORIAL ASSISTANT: Ian Wilker
PICTURE RESEARCH: Patricia Burns
DESIGNER: Diana Blume

Copyright © 1992 by Chelsea House Publishers, a division of Main Line Book Co. All rights reserved. Printed and bound in the United States of America.

First Printing

1  3  5  7  9  8  6  4  2

**Library of Congress Cataloging-in-Publication Data**
LeVert, Suzanne
    Let's discover Canada. New Brunswick/by Suzanne LeVert; George Sheppard, general editor.
p.  cm.
    Includes bibliographical references.
    Includes index.
    Summary: Illustrated text explores the history, geography, and culture of New Brunswick.
    ISBN 0-7910-1029-5
    1. New Brunswick—Juvenile literature.    [1. New Brunswick.]   I. Sheppard. George C. B.
II. Title                                                           90-46039
F1042.4.L48   1991                                                        CIP
971.5'1—dc20                                                              AC

# Contents

# My Canada

## by Pierre Berton

"Nobody knows my country," a great Canadian journalist, Bruce Hutchison, wrote almost half a century ago. It is still true. Most Americans, I think, see Canada as a pleasant vacationland and not much more. And yet we are the United States's greatest single commercial customer, and the United States is our largest customer.

Lacking a major movie industry, we have made no wide-screen epics to chronicle our triumphs and our tragedies. But then there has been little blood in our colonial past—no revolutions, no civil war, not even a wild west. Yet our history is crammed with remarkable men and women. I am thinking of Joshua Slocum, the first man to sail alone around the world, and Robert Henderson, the prospector who helped start the Klondike gold rush. I am thinking of some of our famous artists and writers—comedian Dan Aykroyd, novelists Margaret Atwood and Robertson Davies, such popular performers as Michael J. Fox, Anne Murray, Gordon Lightfoot, and k.d. lang, and hockey greats from Maurice Richard to Gordie Howe to Wayne Gretzky.

The real shape of Canada explains why our greatest epic has been the building of the Pacific Railway to unite the nation from

sea to sea in 1885. On the map, the country looks square. But because the overwhelming majority of Canadians live within 100 miles (160 kilometers) of the U.S. border, in practical terms the nation is long and skinny. We are in fact an archipelago of population islands separated by implacable barriers—the angry ocean, three mountain walls, and the Canadian Shield, that vast desert of billion-year-old rock that sprawls over half the country, rich in mineral treasures, impossible for agriculture.

Canada's geography makes the country difficult to govern and explains our obsession with transportation and communication. The government has to be as involved in railways, airlines, and broadcasting networks as it is with social services such as universal medical care. Rugged individualism is not a Canadian quality. Given the environment, people long ago learned to work together for security.

It is ironic that the very bulwarks that separate us—the chiseled peaks of the Selkirk Mountains, the gnarled scarps north of Lake Superior, the ice-choked waters of the Northumberland Strait —should also be among our greatest attractions for tourists and artists. But if that is the paradox of Canada, it is also the glory.

Grand Manan, the largest of the Fundy Isles, has offered solitude and inspiration to many painters and writers. Although part of the island is wild and uninhabited, lively fishing towns and tourist resorts are found on its shores.

# NEW BRUNSWICK

QUEBEC

Dalhousie

CHALEUR BAY

Campbellton

RESTIGOUCHE
UPLANDS

Caraquet

Shippegan

Edmundston

Mt. Carleton ▲

*Nepisiguit* R.

Bathurst

GULF OF
ST. LAWRENCE

*NW Miramichi* R.

Chatham

MIRAMICHI
BAY

*Little SW Miramichi* R.

Grand Falls

Newcastle

PRINCE EDWARD
ISLAND

MIRAMICHI
BASIN

*SW Miramichi*

NORTHUMBERLAND STRAIT

MAINE

*Saint John* R.

Moncton

Fredericton ★

*Petitcodiac* R.

Oromocto

*St. Croix* R.

Saint John

BAY OF FUNDY

NOVA SCOTIA

DEER ISLAND

CAMPOBELLO
ISLAND

GRAND MANAN

CANADA

UNITED
STATES

| Provincial capital | ★ |
| Cities/Towns | ● |

Kilometers

0   25   50   75   100

25   50

Miles

Purple violet

Black-capped chickadee

# New Brunswick at a Glance

**Area:** 28,354 square miles (73,437 square kilometers)

**Population:** 709,442 (1986 census)

**Capital:** Fredericton (population 44,000)

**Other cities:** Saint John (pop. 76,000), Moncton (pop. 55,000)

**Major rivers:** Saint John, Petitcodiac, Miramichi, Restigouche

**Highest point:** Mt. Carleton, 2,690 feet (815 meters)

**Principal products:** Forestry products (lumber and wood pulp), fish and shellfish, ships, lead, antimony, bismuth, potatoes

**Entered Dominion of Canada:** July 1, 1867

**Motto:** *Spem reduxit* ("Hope was restored")

**Provincial flower:** Purple violet

**Provincial bird:** Black-capped chickadee

**Provincial flag:** Adopted in 1965; shows golden lion on red field at top; below is golden field with oared galley above blue and white stripes that represent the sea

**Government:** Parliamentary system with a single-chambered legislature of 58 members, popularly elected by district for terms of 5 years; the formal head of government is the lieutenant governor, appointed by the federal government as representative of the British crown; the chief executive officer is the premier, head of the ruling party; the premier appoints an executive council from the legislative assembly; New Brunswick is represented in the federal government in Ottawa by 10 senators and 10 members of the House of Commons

# The Land

Located on the Atlantic Ocean coast in southeastern Canada, New Brunswick is called the Picture Province because of the scenic coastline that extends 600 miles (960 kilometers), more than halfway around the province. New Brunswick is one of the four Atlantic provinces of Canada; the others are Newfoundland, Prince Edward Island, and Nova Scotia. Three of the Atlantic provinces—New Brunswick, Prince Edward Island, and Nova Scotia—are sometimes called the Maritime Provinces or the Maritimes ("maritime" means having to do with the sea). New Brunswick is the land link between the other Maritime Provinces and mainland Canada.

The province is about 190 miles (304 kilometers) from north to south and 160 miles (256 kilometers) from east to west, with an area of 28,354 square miles (73,437 square kilometers). It is bounded on the west by Maine in the United States and on the north by the province of Quebec and by Chaleur Bay. On the east, it is bordered by the Gulf of St. Lawrence and the Northumberland Strait, a narrow channel that separates New

*Opposite:* The north-central part of the province consists of low but rugged hills and dense forest. Countless streams race toward the rivers and the sea. *Above:* On the island of Grand Manan, a tranquil meadow overlooks the Bay of Fundy, where the tides are the highest in the world.

Brunswick from Prince Edward Island. On the southeast, it is joined to the province of Nova Scotia by a 15-mile-wide (24-kilometer-wide) strip of land called the Isthmus of Chignecto. On the south, New Brunswick is bounded by the Bay of Fundy.

## Regions and Landscapes

In the western part of the province, the Saint John River flows from northern Maine into New Brunswick and continues south through the province into the Bay of Fundy. Fredericton, the capital, is located on the Saint John River in the center of the province. Edmunston, the largest community in northwestern New Brunswick, is also situated on the Saint John. The north-central part of New Brunswick is called the Restigouche Uplands. The coast of Chaleur Bay is low-lying and gentle; inland, however, the Uplands are hilly and rugged. This region contains New Brunswick's highest point, Mt. Carleton, which at 2,690 feet (815 meters) is one of the tallest peaks in the Atlantic provinces. South of the Uplands, in the center of the province, is the Miramichi Basin, a forested, sparsely inhabited district threaded by many rivers and streams. Newcastle and Chatham are the largest towns in the Miramichi Basin.

The northeastern corner of the province is often called the Acadian Coast, because it was once part of the region called Acadia by early settlers. The Acadian Coast is primarily a fishing district, washed by the waters of Chaleur Bay (the name is French for "bay of warmth" and refers to the mild temperature of the water) and the Gulf of St. Lawrence. The principal communities are small seaports such as Bathurst and Caraquet. The southeastern part of New Brunswick is a stubby peninsula with two distinct seacoasts. On the north is the Northumberland Strait, bordered by lowland marshes, sand dunes, and wide beaches. In summer, the waters of the strait are among Canada's warmest. The beaches are crowded, and the lobster catch is enormous. On the south side of the peninsula is the chilly Bay of Fundy. Moncton, located on the Petitcodiac River, is the biggest city in southeastern New Brunswick.

People walking the sands of the Bay of Fundy at Hopewell Cape are dwarfed by the towering rocks that have been carved out over the centuries by the bay's 52.5-foot (16-meter) tides. The tide is out, but in a little more than 12 hours the water will reach the roots of the trees on top of the rocks.

## The Bay of Fundy

The Bay of Fundy contains two of New Brunswick's most notable geographic features. One is the Fundy Isles. Farthest from the mainland, Grand Manan is the largest island, with an area of 55 square miles (142 square kilometers). Grand Manan has been a retreat for many writers and painters. Campobello Island is the site of the summer home of Franklin D. Roosevelt, who was president of the United States from 1933 to 1945. His estate has been preserved as a museum and park. A fishing colony was first established at Deer Island, the smallest of the islands, in 1783. Fishing and lobstering still form the mainstay of the island's economy, as on the other Fundy Isles.

The other remarkable feature of the Bay of Fundy is its huge tides, which are the highest in the world. Tides are the regular risings and fallings that occur in the oceans because of the gravitational pull of the sun and moon on the water. Nowhere on the planet does the sea rise and fall as dramatically as at the eastern end of the Bay of Fundy. Twice daily, the tide pours into the head of the funnel-shaped bay, raising the water level by as much as 52.5 feet (16 meters) in about 6 hours. Then it reverses and drains back out to sea, only to rush in again when the tide turns once more. So powerful is the incoming tide that it pushes back the water flowing to the sea from the Saint John and Petitcodiac rivers, and for a short time twice each day, these rivers actually flow upstream. The Bay of Fundy tides provide New Brunswick with more than an interesting tourist attraction. They also keep the eastern harbors clear of ice, allowing the city of Saint John, situated at the mouth of the Saint John River, to function as one of Canada's chief winter seaports. A number of plans to harness the tides to produce electrical power have been considered, but so far none has been carried out.

## Land, Forest, and Water

The rocky soils of northern and western New Brunswick contain stores of minerals, especially zinc, copper, and lead. The central and eastern parts of the province have deposits of coal, limestone, gypsum, and oil-bearing shale. Most of New Brunswick's soil is not well suited for farming. The best farmland is located along the rivers in central and southern New Brunswick. Along the upper portion of the Saint John River, the soil is rich in lime, which makes it perfect for growing potatoes, the province's chief crop. The lowland plains along the Bay of Fundy coast are also farmed. Forests cover approximately 90 percent of the province's land area, making New Brunswick one of the most densely forested regions in the world. The province's forests contain a mixed growth of hard and soft woods, including spruce, fir, cedar, maple, poplar, white pine, jack pine, red pine, hemlock, and larch. The northeast coast has peat bogs, which are damp areas where moss and other vegetation has been compressed over centuries into a substance called peat. The peat can be cut into bricks, dried, and burned for fuel, like coal.

Most of New Brunswick's wildlife is found in the forests. Native animals include moose, black bears, wildcats, deer, woodchucks, muskrat, beavers, raccoons, foxes, skunks, weasels, mink, rabbits, and squirrels. Several hundred varieties of birds either live in New Brunswick or pass through the province yearly on their migrations. Seabirds, including the increasingly rare puffin, nest in colonies on Grand Manan and other coastal islands. Marine life includes river trout and Atlantic salmon, lobsters, clams and oysters, sardines, cod, and herring. Several species of whales frequent the offshore waters, and whale-watching tours are a fast-growing local industry.

New Brunswick's most important river is the 418-mile-long (668-kilometer-long) Saint John. For decades, it was a highway

The best farmland in the province is found in the broad valley of the Saint John River. Most of New Brunswick, however, is not well suited to agriculture.

The puffin, a seabird that nests on offshore rocks and islands in the North Atlantic Ocean, feeds on fish. It may be facing a serious food shortage because of intensive fishing by commercial fleets in its home waters.

into Canada's interior; today it is an energy source. At Grand Falls, about 225 miles (360 kilometers) inland from the Bay of Fundy, the Saint John drops 75 feet (23 meters) over a magnificent waterfall. A hydroelectric power plant there produces electricity, and other such plants are located downstream.

## Climate and Weather

New Brunswick has a continental climate, with cold winters and warm summers. Winter hits hardest in the northwestern highlands, where temperatures average about 10 degrees Fahrenheit (−11 degrees Celsius) and snowfall is heavy. This is the coolest part of the province even in the summer. July temperatures average about 65°F (18°C), although some of the interior valleys get much hotter. Frost may occur in the northwest during any month of the year. The climate of the southeast, especially the coast, is a bit warmer. January temperatures there average about 20°F (−6°C), and July temperatures average about 70°F (20°C). Each year the province receives about 40 inches (102 centimeters) of precipitation, half of which falls as rain during the warmer months, and the other half of which falls as winter snow.

# The History

For centuries before European explorers arrived, present-day New Brunswick was inhabited by two groups of Native Americans, the Micmac and the Malecite.

The Micmac numbered about 20,000 and lived along the east coast of North America, from Massachusetts to Quebec. In New Brunswick, they lived north and east of the Saint John River. Each year, they migrated twice, moving into the forests to hunt deer during the winter and gathering on the ocean shore to fish during the summer. Micmac culture emphasized painting, music, and fine crafts, including elaborate stitchery and beadwork.

The Malecite lived west of the Micmac. They were more settled than the Micmac, and their numbers were far fewer. Small bands of Malecite lived along the Saint John River in New Brunswick and Maine. They were farmers, cultivating corn and vegetables in addition to hunting and fishing. Like the Micmac, the Malecite were talented craftspeople. They lived in tents made of painted animal skins and navigated the river in intricately decorated birch-bark canoes.

*Opposite:* French explorer Jacques Cartier was the first European known to have visited the shores of New Brunswick. He sailed along the coast in 1534.
*Above:* An elderly Micmac woman, photographed around the beginning of the 20th century. The Micmac and the Malecite were the two Native peoples who lived in New Brunswick before the Europeans arrived.

## Acadia Is Born

Viking adventurers may have glimpsed New Brunswick's shores from the decks of their longboats as early as the 11th century, but the first European explorer who is known to have landed there was a 35-year-old Frenchman named Jacques Cartier (1491–1557). Cartier was trying to find a sea passage through North America to Asia when he sailed along the northern shore of New Brunswick in the summer of 1534. He probably traded for food with the Micmac before sailing on to explore the mouth of the St. Lawrence River. Legend says that 70 years later, in 1604, when the explorers Samuel de Champlain and Pierre de Guast arrived in the area, they were greeted on the beach by an elderly Native chieftain who remembered Cartier.

When cartographers drew their first maps of this newly discovered territory, they referred to the east coast of present-day Canada as Arcadia. The Atlantic coast near present-day Delaware had been named Arcadia by Giovanni da Verrazano, an Italian explorer in the service of France, and mapmakers mistakenly shifted the location of Arcadia to the north. However, the name stuck, and the *r* was eventually dropped. The region around the Gulf of St. Lawrence became known as Acadia, or *Acadie* in French.

The boundaries of Acadia have never been clearly defined. At first the name was given to most of the northeast coast of North America; Prince Edward Island and part of Maine were often considered part of Acadia. But the name referred in particular to the territory that now makes up Nova Scotia and New Brunswick. Cartier claimed this region for France, but the first settlers did not arrive until the early 17th century. By that time, the British had begun to stake claims to some of the same territory, making France determined to settle the land and thereby keep it under French control. King Henry IV of France commissioned an expedition to chart Acadia and find a suitable spot for settlement; this is the expedition that arrived in New Brunswick in 1604, led by Champlain and Guast. Their ships entered the mouth of a large river on June 4, which to Roman

Samuel de Champlain was one of the founders of the first French settlement in what is now New Brunswick. He nearly perished during the first hard winter in the new land.

Catholics is the feast day of St. John the Baptist, so Guast named it the Saint John River. His first choice for a permanent settlement was Île de St. Croix, a small island at the mouth of the St. Croix River. The choice was an unfortunate one. While Guast sailed back to France to fetch more settlers, Champlain and 79 other men braved a long, hard winter on the desolate island. Unable to cross the icy strait that separated them from the mainland, almost half the party died of scurvy (a vitamin-deficiency disease) or starvation before the spring thaw.

The following summer, the remaining settlers moved to Port-Royal in present-day Nova Scotia, where they were soon joined by newcomers from France. Acadia was slowly colonized by small communities of intrepid French pioneers, who endured many hardships in the rugged land. These early settlements were largely ignored by the French government, which was more concerned with other New World colonies. The first Acadians were therefore forced to rely on their own resources. Because of their isolation and independence, they developed a close-knit society, with its own traditions, values, and even its own

During the 17th century, hardy pioneers—mostly from France—carved isolated homesteads and small communities out of the dense forest. They called the region Acadia.

language, a dialect of French. Free-spirited and hardy, the Acadians hunted and fished, farmed and raised livestock, and defied the French government by trading with the British settlers in Maine and New England.

## Early Days

The Acadians would probably not have survived without the aid and friendship of the Micmac and the Malecite. The Natives helped the settlers build homes and taught them how to farm and fish in Acadia's climate. Later, the Natives fought alongside the French to protect Acadia from British encroachment.

Unfortunately, contact with the Europeans was not always beneficial to the Natives. The Europeans brought with them diseases against which the Natives had never developed immunities, and smallpox and measles ravaged many Native communities well into the 19th century. In addition, the Natives became economically dependent on the settlers, neglecting their own cultures and livelihoods to trade for European goods. Finally, as more and more Europeans arrived, the Natives were pushed off their land to make room for the settlers. The first reserves for Native Americans in all of North America were established in New Brunswick, and the Micmac and Malecite were eventually forced to live in the most isolated and barren areas of the province.

Acadia's first profitable economic venture, however, depended upon cooperation between Natives and Europeans. The Acadian forests were full of fur-bearing animals, such as beavers and mink, whose pelts fetched high prices in Europe, and the Natives were eager to trap these animals and trade their furs for tools, blankets, liquor, and other goods. Soon the fur trade flourished in the Maritime Provinces. Farming and the construction of permanent settlements were neglected in favor of the more profitable fur trade.

THE COMMUNITY SCHOOL
St. Louis, Mo.
Fifth Grade Library

When the British gained control of Acadia, they feared an uprising by the French settlers. To prevent such an occurrence, the British governor ordered the Acadians deported in 1755. Thousands of them were driven from their homes into exile.

Sir Thomas Carleton, the British governor of New Brunswick, settled a border dispute with the neighboring province of Quebec by playing a dice game with Quebec's governor. Carleton won, and New Brunswick kept the territory that Quebec had coveted.

Because the French failed to settle the region rapidly and in large numbers, Acadia was open to attack and conquest by the expanding British Empire. Although it was still largely wilderness, Acadia became a crucial battleground in the long struggle between the French and the British for dominance in North America. Throughout the 17th and 18th centuries, control of the present-day provinces of Nova Scotia and New Brunswick passed back and forth between these two world powers.

During this period, communities developed in New Brunswick. Some Acadians settled on the Isthmus of Chignecto and devised farming methods that enabled them to grow crops in the salty tidal marshes of the Bay of Fundy. Near the mouth of the Saint John River, fur trader Charles La Tour built a fort that eventually became the city of Saint John. And about 70 miles (112 kilometers) upstream, another Acadian settlement sprang up where a stream called the Nashwaak River meets the Saint John. In 1691, the French governor of Acadia established the colony's capital there and built Fort Nashwaak to defend the area from the British. Fredericton, the capital of New Brunswick, was later built on the site of Fort Nashwaak.

In 1713, the Treaty of Utrecht ended a long and bitter war among the nations of Europe, and France was forced to turn over some of its colonial holdings to Britain. Acadia became a British territory, and its new owners immediately renamed it Nova Scotia, meaning New Scotland. But because Acadia's precise boundaries had never been defined, France claimed that part of it (the present-day province of New Brunswick) was still French territory, and the struggle between the two powers continued.

At first, the British paid little attention to Nova Scotia, being more concerned with the New England colonies. Few British settlers came to Acadia in the early 18th century. Fearing a revolt by the French Acadians in the region, the British overlords tried to make the Acadian settlers take an oath of loyalty to the British government. The Acadians refused, promising only to remain neutral in the seemingly endless power struggle. For a time, this compromise was accepted. But later, when the French had regained some territory in nearby Newfoundland, the British decided to act. They brought numerous settlers into the territory—about 7,000 British colonists, mostly from New England, arrived in Nova Scotia in the 1750s. And when war broke out once more between France and England, the British again demanded that the Acadians swear an oath of loyalty. They refused, and the English governor of the colony, Charles Lawrence, expelled them from the colony in 1755. Every Acadian who could be rounded up was deported to England or to a British colony. Some Acadians escaped to Quebec or hid in remote parts of Acadia. In 1763, another European treaty—the Treaty of Paris—ended French rule in Canada. By that time, more than 13,000 Acadians had been deported or displaced from their land. Some went to present-day Louisiana, where they became the source of the Cajun (from "Acadian") culture. Others managed to return quietly to Acadia during the following decades, settling along New Brunswick's northeastern shore.

## British Rule

Once the British power in Canada was restored, many new colonists began to arrive. The first permanent British settlement in the part of the Nova Scotia colony that is now New Brunswick was established in 1762 by settlers from the Massachusetts colony. During the American Revolution, which began in 1775, some of these settlers sympathized with the rebels and even attacked British posts in Nova Scotia. But the British influence in New Brunswick was strengthened by Scottish immigrants who began to settle along the valley of the Miramichi River in the mid-1760s. And at the close of the American Revolution, Nova Scotia received another influx of settlers—approximately 14,000 men and women from the former British colonies that had just won their independence as the United States. Called Loyalists because they were still loyal to the British crown, these newcomers came to Nova Scotia because it remained in British hands. Thousands of Loyalists landed at the mouth of the Saint John River and found themselves surrounded by a wilderness of

Thousands of British Loyalists who fled the United States after the American Revolution settled in New Brunswick. They landed on a barren shore, but before long they had built cities and towns.

rocks, trees, and water. Some Loyalists perished of cold and hunger, but the hardy survivors built Fredericton and Saint John, two of Canada's oldest cities.

Nova Scotia's population soared with the arrival of the Loyalists, and the colonists urged the Colonial Office in London to divide Nova Scotia into two colonies. Their request was granted, and New Brunswick was named a separate colony in 1784. By this time, British influence dominated much of the colony. Many French and Native place names had been replaced by English ones, and the public buildings, squares, and houses of the growing towns were built in the British style. The colony was also developing a new industry based on New Brunswick's chief resource—trees. The forests were filled with the white pine that was favored by shipbuilders. Conflict arose over the densely wooded northwestern corner of New Brunswick, the heart of the

Logging was the mainstay of New Brunswick's economy during the early 19th century. Most of the timber was used for shipbuilding.

logging industry. It was claimed by New Brunswick, Quebec, and the United States. Sir Thomas Carleton, the British governor of New Brunswick, is said to have settled the dispute with Quebec by throwing dice with that colony's governor. Carleton won, and Quebec gave up its claim. But the border between Maine and New Brunswick remained in dispute until 1842, when the United States finally withdrew its claim.

The economy of New Brunswick boomed in the early years of the 19th century. Immigrants arrived seeking jobs and new lives. Many of them came from Scotland and Ireland; during the first half of the 19th century, the Scots and Irish outnumbered the English in New Brunswick. By the middle of the century, the colony's population had climbed to more than 200,000.

Saint John benefited from the shipbuilding boom because of its position on the Saint John River. Logs cut in the northwestern forests could be made into rafts and sent downriver to the city, where they were processed into lumber in newly constructed sawmills and lumberyards. By the 1840s, Saint John rivaled Quebec as one of the principal shipbuilding centers of North America.

## Confederation

By the mid-19th century, other British colonies in Canada had gained in both population size and economic power. Some of the provinces began to debate the formation of a union, or confederation, that would give the colonies greater protection against encroachment or attack by other powers, such as the United States. Confederation would also increase and consolidate the colonies' economic and political power. Alone, each colony was relatively insignificant, but together they could form a more impressive and influential body. At first, the three maritime colonies—Prince Edward Island, Nova Scotia, and New Brunswick—considered forming their own union. Then the two biggest and richest colonies, Canada East (present-day Quebec) and Canada West (present-day Ontario), suggested a larger union. After much discussion, four of the colonies—Quebec,

Ontario, Nova Scotia, and New Brunswick—united in a confederation and formed the Dominion of Canada in 1867. Prince Edward Island later joined, as did other provinces in western Canada.

The confederation—and Canada's new railways—brought a surge of population and economic growth to New Brunswick. The New Brunswick section of a railway line through the Maritimes was completed in 1876, and the Canadian Pacific Railway, which extended across Canada, reached Saint John in 1889. With the railways came new businesses such as textile mills and iron foundries. It seemed that New Brunswick would become a thriving center of manufacturing and trade.

But political and economic factors would continue to undermine New Brunswick's prosperity well into the 20th century. The shipbuilding industry languished after steam-driven, iron-hulled ships were introduced. At the same time, trade with the United States was greatly reduced because the high tariffs on Canadian goods sold in the United States made Canadian lumber and other products too expensive for some U.S. buyers. In addition, the high cost of shipping goods by rail across Canada caused many businesses to fail. Factories were shut down, unemployment rose, and thousands of workers left the province to find jobs elsewhere.

Toward the end of the 19th century, Canada's western provinces began to gain economic power. This marked the beginning of a steady decline in the economic status of the Maritime Provinces. Grain exports from the prairie provinces of Manitoba, Saskatchewan, and Alberta became far more valuable to the nation than the wood produced by New Brunswick and the other Maritime Provinces. As a result, federal attention and funds were slowly shifted westward. Many of the workers who left New Brunswick in search of better economic opportunities headed for western Canada, the seat of the new prosperity.

## The Twentieth Century

During the 1920s, government agencies studied the growing disparity in economic well-being between the Maritimes and

Canadian painter Robert Harris's *Fathers of the Confederation* depicts the meeting that led to the unification of the Canadian colonies. New Brunswick was one of the first four colonies to join the Confederation.

other Canadian provinces. But before any corrective action could be taken, Canada's economy was devastated by the worldwide Great Depression of the 1930s. World War II (1939–45) followed, and New Brunswick's economy remained stagnant for decades. Even during and after World War II, when many other areas experienced economic growth, New Brunswick and the other Maritime Provinces remained economically depressed. Social services such as education and health care suffered from a lack of funds; the illiteracy and infant mortality rates were the highest in Canada during the 1940s and 1950s.

New Brunswick's problems were complicated by its having, in effect, two separate societies. In the north and east were the French-speaking Acadians, who lived in tiny rural villages, lacked sufficient job opportunities, and were generally far poorer than the English-speaking inhabitants of the province. Most of the English-speaking population lived in and around Saint John and Fredericton in the southern part of the province, where they had access to better jobs and social services.

The province's economic and social conditions began to improve when a dynamic Acadian politician named Louis Joseph Robichaud was elected premier of the province in 1960. Working toward the goal of equal opportunity for all citizens, he and his administration passed more than 125 new laws during 10 years in office. These laws were designed to boost the provincial economy and to distribute opportunities and services more

Louis Joseph Robichaud (left) became premier of New Brunswick in 1960; he was the first Acadian to be elected to that post. He is shown with Pierre Trudeau, Canada's prime minister from 1968 to 1979 and again from 1980 to 1984.

equally between English-speaking inhabitants and Acadians. One of the first steps taken by the Robichaud administration was the reorganization and centralization of the provincial government. Traditionally each of the 15 counties in the province was responsible for providing its inhabitants with health care, education, and a judicial system. People who lived in the poorer counties received fewer and less adequate social services than those who lived in more prosperous counties. Robichaud changed the system so that the central provincial government would be responsible for providing effective social services for all citizens.

At the same time, massive plans for economic development were started by both the provincial and the federal administrations. Hydroelectric power plants were built, the forestry and mining industries were expanded, and major highways were constructed during the 1960s and 1970s. The province's economic and social conditions were greatly improved by these reforms.

## New Brunswick Today

Because of its small size and population—709,442 inhabitants in an area of 28,354 square miles (73,437 square kilometers), according to Canada's 1986 census—New Brunswick has often been on the outer fringe of national political life. At the beginning of the 1990s, however, New Brunswick made national headlines by proposing a change in the Meech Lake Accord. The accord was a proposed amendment to Canada's constitution that would grant special status to the province of Quebec because of its distinctly French culture. Although Quebec's French-speaking people strongly supported the Meech Lake Accord, the proposal angered many other Canadians—especially the Native Americans and the Acadians, who felt that if the French of Quebec deserved special recognition, so did they. In the spring of 1990, Frank McKenna, who was then premier of New Brunswick, suggested that the Meech Lake Accord should protect the rights and cultural integrity of *all* of Canada's minorities, not just the Quebec French. Although the accord did not become law, McKenna's proposal brought nationwide attention to New Brunswick.

Today, New Brunswick's education system, health care, and other social services are comparable to those of most other provinces. But a number of challenges remain. The unemployment rate remains high—approximately 15 percent of workers do not have jobs. The average income in the province, about $10,500 per person, is well below the national average. And the Acadians and Native Americans, the two largest minority groups in New Brunswick, are still excluded in many ways from the province's political and economic mainstream. New Brunswick's leaders hope to strengthen the province's economy and to make New Brunswick a more powerful presence in national affairs. How the province meets these challenges will determine its fortunes in the 1990s and beyond.

# The Economy

Until recently, natural resources such as fur, fish, and wood were the mainstay of New Brunswick's economy. Since the mid-20th century, however, the province has tried to broaden its economic base. Mining, agriculture, manufacturing, and services such as communications, tourism, transportation, and finance are now a significant part of the provincial economy.

    The service industries—banks, hotels, restaurants, insurance companies, and the like—are the province's principal employers, accounting for nearly 60 percent of all jobs. Tourism is one such industry that has gained considerable importance. In the 1980s, New Brunswick launched a major campaign to attract visitors. Now tourists from other countries and from elsewhere in Canada bring about $450 million in income to New Brunswick each year. Visitors who are interested in art and history are attracted to New Brunswick's many museums and re-created historical villages, but it is the province's natural wonders that draw most of the tourists. New Brunswick's two national parks, Fundy and Kouchibouguac, have more than 2.5 million visitors annually.

About 6,500 New Brunswickers work on fishing boats; another 10,000 work in fish-processing plants. Fishermen on Grand Manan (opposite) haul in a net. Crabmeat is packed in a plant in Cap-Pelé (above).

Shipbuilding—particularly the manufacture of military patrol boats—is an important part of the provincial economy.

## Manufacturing

Manufacturing accounts for 14 percent of the province's annual gross domestic product (GDP) of $4.5 billion; this sector of the economy employs about 40,000 people. Food and beverage processing is the province's largest industry, followed by the processing of wood products.

Close to 10,000 workers are employed by approximately 130 fish-processing plants, including a herring plant and a tuna plant in St. Andrews. Agricultural products such as potatoes and vegetables are processed in plants located near the farms, notably in the towns of Florenceville and Grand Falls. Dairy products such as butter and cheese are processed in Sussex.

The Saint John Shipbuilding and Dry Dock Company is one of the largest employers in Saint John. The company was once an offshoot of the forestry industry, using white pine from New Brunswick's forests, but the ships it makes today are built of steel, not of wood. Saint John Shipbuilding is one of Canada's leading manufacturers of military ships; in 1983, the company received a government contract worth almost $3 billion for the manufacture of patrol frigates. That contract was extended in late 1987, significantly improving the economic prospects of Saint John and of the entire province.

Mineral processing is another local resource-based industry. An oil refinery at Saint John, a mining and smelting operation at Bathurst, and a lead smelter at Belledune process minerals mined in New Brunswick as well as those imported from other provinces and countries.

The construction industry employs about 17,000 people and contributes approximately $1 billion to the province's economic production each year. Throughout most of the 1980s, a nuclear plant at Point Lepreau was the largest project under construction. During the 1990s, construction will focus on the modernization of the province's aging industrial plants, especially many of its pulp-and-paper mills.

## Forestry

The forestry industry accounts for 15 percent of the province's jobs, 60 percent of its exports, and more than 25 percent of the goods produced in New Brunswick. Approximately 80 percent of the timber that is harvested is processed into wood pulp. Near Saint John, a company called the Irving Group operates three large pulp mills that produce newsprint, tissue, and material for corrugated cardboard boxes. The New Brunswick International Paper Company operates a newsprint mill at Dalhousie. The 20 percent of New Brunswick's harvested timber that is not processed into pulp or paper is made into lumber and wood products.

More than half of the province's productive forest land is privately owned. The rest is owned by the government and leased to large firms. Forest conservation is of prime importance to the people of New Brunswick. Not only does forestry depend upon the continued survival of the forests, but the province's large stretches of undeveloped forest attract many hunters, campers, hikers, and nature lovers to New Brunswick, accounting for a significant portion of the income from tourism. Efforts to prevent forest fires, to control insects, and to replant forests have had some success in recent years, but overharvesting has reduced the total productive forest area by at least five percent since 1979. Other threats to the forests include the budworm, a destructive moth larva that devours spruce and fir needles, and acid rain.

## Mining

About 4,000 people are employed in New Brunswick's mining industry. Mining was relatively unimportant to the provincial economy until the mid-1950s, when large reserves of base metals were discovered in the northern part of the province, around Bathurst. New Brunswick is now responsible for a significant share of Canada's mineral production, including zinc, silver, lead, copper, antimony, and bismuth. Mining accounts for $500 million in earnings each year and has brought jobs and income to

Forestry was New Brunswick's leading industry in the early 19th century. Today the forestry trade employs about 15 percent of the province's workers and produces 60 percent of its exports.

Bathurst, in the northeast, is the center of New Brunswick's mining industry. The world's largest zinc mines are located here.

some of the most economically depressed regions of New Brunswick. New Brunswick has one of Canada's very few sources of antimony, a mineral used in medicines, matches, and fire-proofing materials. Currently, New Brunswick produces about 85 percent of the nation's antimony. Another rare metal is bismuth, used in making metal alloys. New Brunswick is the source of 70 percent of Canada's bismuth.

## Agriculture

Agriculture has declined in New Brunswick, as it has elsewhere in Canada, since the mid-20th century. In 1951, about 27,000 people worked on farms; in 1986, only 6,000 people worked the land. During that same period, the amount of cultivated land was reduced by almost half. Currently only about 5 percent of the province is farmland. The farms are generally small, averaging less than 250 acres (100 hectares) in size.

Nevertheless, New Brunswick produces approximately $120 million worth of agricultural goods each year. Potatoes are the principal cash crop, and New Brunswick seed potatoes (those used to start potato crops elsewhere) are sold around the world, accounting for 20 percent of all seed potatoes grown in Canada. Dairying is also important, with butter, cheese, and condensed

Dulse is a New Brunswick delicacy. It is a seaweed that is dried in the sun and eaten as a crisp, salty snack or pickled and used as a relish.

milk being the principal products. Together, dairy products and potatoes account for about 44 percent of the province's total agricultural production. Beef, poultry, and hogs make up another 31 percent of New Brunswick's agricultural production, and field crops of fruit and vegetables contribute another 8 percent. Eggs and maple products, including some of the finest-quality maple syrup produced in North America, make up the remainder.

Two New Brunswick delicacies are fiddlehead ferns and dulse. The ferns grow along the province's streams. Gathered in the spring, they are boiled and served with lemon and butter. Dulse is a seaweed that is harvested off the coast, especially in the town of Dark Harbour on Grand Manan. The salty weed is dried in the sun and eaten as a snack, like potato chips.

## Fishing

New Brunswick ranks fourth among the Canadian provinces in the total value of fish caught. It accounts for 18 percent of the production of Canadian east coast fisheries. New Brunswick's fishing industry declined steadily until the 1960s; during the 1970s and 1980s it revived somewhat when fishing vessels and methods were modernized. Each year, 6,500 fishermen operating almost 4,000 vessels catch fish and shellfish worth more than $90 million. Yet the fishing industry remains depressed, and the rate of unemployment has climbed to more than 40 percent in some fishing villages.

One problem confronting the fishing industry is large-scale overfishing by huge, mechanized commercial fleets from both Canada and the United States. Overfishing has seriously reduced the numbers of many commercially valuable fish and shellfish, such as salmon, groundfish, and lobsters. Plans are under way to increase fish-farming—that is, the controlled breeding and harvesting of food fish—which has already become a $70 million industry in the Bay of Fundy region.

Lobster is the major catch of New Brunswick's fishing industry, accounting for almost one-third of the value of all seafood harvested. Lobsters are caught in the Northumberland Strait, one of the richest lobster breeding grounds in the world. Crabs are also caught in the strait; the annual crab catch is worth about $17 million. Herring are found in abundance in New Brunswick's waters because of the Bay of Fundy tides, which carry enormous quantities of the microorganisms called plankton, upon which herring feed. Sardines, which are young herring, are also harvested, as are cod and other groundfish. The world's largest species of tuna, the bluefin, is found in these waters. Bluefin were once the prey of sport fishermen, but now they are caught by commercial fleets. Most of the bluefin catch is exported to Japan. The number of Atlantic salmon has been greatly reduced by overfishing and pollution. Commercial salmon fishing was banned in the 1970s, and federal authorities have established several salmon-rearing stations; one of these stations is among the largest in the world. Economic planners and conservationists alike hope that the population of salmon, as well as that of other forms of marine life whose numbers have dwindled, will increase in New Brunswick's waters.

Wild fiddlehead ferns, boiled and served with butter and lemon, are a spring treat.

# The People

With 709,442 people, New Brunswick has the third smallest population in Canada. Only Prince Edward Island and Newfoundland have fewer inhabitants. But although New Brunswick's population may be small in number, it is rich in cultural diversity. Representatives of the three cultures that founded the Canadian nation—Native Americans, people of French descent, and people of British descent—live in the province.

About 7,000 Natives, members of the Malecite and Micmac tribal nations, live in reserves scattered throughout the northeastern part of the province. Because reserve lands are controlled by the federal government rather than the provincial government, the Natives have been largely excluded from provincial affairs for most of this century, and they have lived in isolation from the rest of New Brunswick society. Recently, however, new social policies and changes in the administration of Native affairs have begun to make it easier for Native Canadians to enter the mainstream of work, education, and political life. But

*Opposite:* The ancestors of this north shore fisherman probably included some Acadians, as the early French settlers were called. Thirty-two percent of the province's inhabitants are of Acadian descent.
*Above:* Flags fly in the harbor of Caraquet, a fishing village on the northeast shore and a center of traditional Acadian culture.

despite these efforts, the average income and the standard of living of the Native population remains, in general, far lower than that of other Canadians. Some New Brunswick Natives have taken the government to court, claiming that land was unfairly taken from the tribes during the early days of European settlement. Such claims and legal cases are being debated throughout Canada, but the Natives have not yet won any victories against the federal or provincial governments in New Brunswick.

The Acadians are the descendants of the province's first European settlers. They constitute about 32 percent of the population—a higher percentage than in any other region inhabited by Acadians. Most of New Brunswick's Acadians live in tiny fishing villages on the northeast coast. Because the Acadians have long been linked to the sea, they have suffered economic setbacks stemming from the overall decline in the fishing industry. Many Acadians have abandoned the sea and now work in mining centers such as Bathurst and Dalhousie.

Compared with the English-speaking people who came to dominate New Brunswick, the Acadians were isolated and poor. They and their unique culture were long ignored by the English-speaking majority. Yet New Brunswick's Acadians had a certain political strength because of their numbers and their cultural unity. Before Acadian Louis Joseph Robichaud was elected premier of the province in 1960, a radical movement urged the Acadians to form a separate society with its own homeland. This movement largely died out when Robichaud's administration succeeded in enacting reforms, which included making the province officially bilingual (with French and English given equal status under the law). The courts and schools now use both French and English, and the Acadians also have their own university, the Université de Moncton, which includes a law school.

English-speaking people make up more than 62 percent of New Brunswick's population. Many of them are descendants of 19th-century immigrants from England, Scotland, and Ireland, including thousands of Irish and Scottish immigrants who came

The people of Saint John celebrate Saint Patrick's Day with a parade and a week-long Irish festival. Many settlers and immigrants from Ireland made their homes in and around Saint John.

to New Brunswick to work in the shipyards. When the shipbuilding industry began to decline during the mid-1800s, economic difficulties combined with age-old religious conflicts between Protestants and Catholics to create an atmosphere of stormy unrest in New Brunswick. Widespread rioting and fighting between immigrant groups occurred, especially in Saint John.

Since that time, however, the people of New Brunswick have lived in relative peace and harmony. Today the cultural contributions of the province's various population groups are enthusiastically celebrated in Saint John: Loyalist Days celebrates the early history of the English and the Loyalists who came to New Brunswick from the United States; the Festival Acadien focuses on New Brunswick's first French-speaking settlers; and St. Patrick's Week observes the province's Irish heritage.

## Education and the Arts

One of the most important reforms enacted during the 1960s was the creation of two separate but equal school systems for the children of New Brunswick: One maintains a curriculum in French and the other in English. The French-speaking schools now have about 45,000 students in grades 1 through 12, and the English-speaking schools have about 92,000. Each school system is headed by its own deputy minister of education and administered by its own set of local school boards.

New Brunswick has postsecondary schools for speakers of both French and English. A total of 10 community colleges serve 4,000 French and 8,000 English students. Among the English-language universities, the University of New Brunswick (UNB) was founded in 1785 and is the oldest institution of higher learning in Canada; it was the site of Canada's first astronomical observatory and its first engineering school. The other English-language universities are Mount Allison University near Moncton, which specializes in fine arts programs, and St. Thomas University in Fredericton, which is affiliated with UNB. The three universities have a total of 14,000 students. Since 1963, the leading French-language university in the Maritimes has been the Université de Moncton. It has branches in the three largely

The University of New Brunswick in Fredericton was founded in 1785, making it Canada's oldest university.

Acadian communities of Moncton, Edmundston, and Shippegan. In addition to liberal arts studies, the university also offers postgraduate programs in law, nursing, and forestry.

Canada's oldest literary magazine, the *Fiddlehead*, is published by the University of New Brunswick. The magazine features work by the province's many poets—so many poets have lived or worked in New Brunswick that it is often called the Poetry Province.

Alden Nowlan (1933–83) was a well-known poet who was at the center of literary life in the Maritimes during the mid-20th century. He published three volumes of poetry, including *Bread, Wine and Salt*, which won the Governor-General's literary award. His collection of stories in the volume *Miracle at Indian River* offers an insider's view of the lives of country folk in the Maritimes. Earlier writers—including Jonathan Odell (1737–1818), Sir Charles Roberts (1860–1943), often considered the father of Canadian literature, and Bliss Carman (1861–1929)—drew upon New Brunswick's landscape, people, and way of life for literary inspiration. Stuart Trueman is a local historian who has written several volumes of New Brunswick lore, and Raymond Fraser, author of *The Black Horse Tavern*, is a contemporary novelist.

Since the 1940s, Mount Allison University has been a haven for New Brunswick's visual artists, especially when Alex Colville taught there from 1946 to 1963. Colville is one of Canada's leading painters. He is best known for a style of painting in which landscapes, animals, and people are represented in a detailed yet exaggerated way. Painters who studied under Colville include John Christopher Pratt and Thomas Forrestall, both of whom are internationally known for their depictions of eastern Canada.

The literary and musical traditions of the Acadians are preserved and encouraged at the Université de Moncton. Its Centre d'Etudes Acadiennes (Center for Acadian Studies) has a section devoted to Acadian folklore, including 300-year-old songs, legends, and traditions. Antoinine Maillet, born in Buctouche, New Brunswick, in 1929, is a well-known novelist who draws upon Acadian language and folklore in her work. Maillet, who won the prestigious French Prix Goncourt literary award for her novel *Pélagie la Charrette*, is at the forefront of modern Acadian literature.

Acadians are also active on the international music scene. Choral music is one of Acadia's best-loved traditions, and most Acadian parishes and schools boast fine choirs and chorales. The choral group of the Université de Moncton has received several awards, and another group called Les Jeunes Chanteurs d'Acadie (Young Acadian Singers), founded in Moncton in 1957, has won many international prizes. Acadian musicians and singers are becoming known far beyond the borders of New Brunswick and Nova Scotia. With 11 albums to her credit, Edith Butler, born near Caraquet, New Brunswick, in 1942, is an internationally popular Acadian singer whose emotional, powerful voice has brought Acadian music and history to the rest of the world.

Acadian and English folk music alike are featured at the Miramichi Folk Festival, held annually in Newcastle. Singers, step-dancers, fiddlers, and other musicians flock from all over eastern Canada to enjoy this celebration of folk traditions.

Theater thrives in New Brunswick in both French and English. The Université de Moncton has an Acadian theater group, and Theatre New Brunswick (TNB) of Fredericton produces original and classical plays and musicals in English. TNB, the only official provincial theater in Canada, is also a touring company, performing throughout the province's cities and towns.

## Sports and Recreation

New Brunswick has no professional sports teams, but amateur athletics—from softball and soccer in the summer to hockey and curling in the winter—are enjoyed throughout the province. Hockey, Canada's favorite pastime, is the most popular sport in the province. Many youngsters born in New Brunswick spend their childhood playing hockey with friends and on junior teams, and some have gone on to play in the National Hockey League.

Curling is another team sport played on ice. This game of Scottish origin involves propelling granite stones along a 138-foot (42-meter) lane of ice. Players compete to see who can hit, or get nearest to, a target at the other end of the lane. In many provinces, curling is second only to hockey as a favorite winter sport for both spectators and participants.

Less competitive athletes can find many opportunities for exercise and enjoyment in New Brunswick. The province's parks attract hikers, campers, skiers, hunters, and bird-watchers. Boating on the province's many lakes and off the coast is a popular summer pastime; so are fishing and wind surfing. The province also has more than 30 golf courses.

Campers enjoy a meal and a waterfront view in Kouchibouguac National Park on the Gulf of Saint Lawrence. The province's unspoiled wilderness provides opportunities for outdoor adventures that appeal to residents and tourists alike.

# The Cities and Towns

## Fredericton

Named for Frederick, the second son of the English king George III (1738–1820), Fredericton was made the capital when the colony of New Brunswick was officially created in 1784 and has remained the capital ever since. It is sometimes called the City of Stately Elms because it is one of the most elegant capitals in eastern Canada. Located on the banks of the Saint John River, Fredericton is known for its quiet tree-lined streets and handsome Victorian mansions, direct links with its history.

Fredericton now has a very British appearance, but for a brief period in the 1690s it was the capital of French Acadia, called St. Anne's Point and later Fort Nashwaak. It was from this site close to the Maine border that the French launched several attacks upon British settlements in New England. Later, when the British won control of Acadia, they took revenge by burning the small village that still stood on the site of Fort Nashwaak. In its place, they built the city now called Fredericton. Many of the homes and public buildings were designed and built by wealthy, cultivated Loyalists who fled the American Revolution and settled in New Brunswick, hoping to re-create a distinctly British way of life.

*Opposite:* Saint John is New Brunswick's largest city, with a population of 76,000. It is a shipbuilding center and also a year-round port for international shipping.
*Above:* The Provincial Legislature in Fredericton, the capital, was built in 1880 and is the seat of the province's government.

Life in modern Fredericton is still shaped by many of the original British institutions, founded during the early years of colonial history. One such institution is the University of New Brunswick, located on a hill overlooking the city. In 1785, the British founded it under the name King's College. Over time, it grew into one of the most prestigious institutions in the Maritimes. It now enrolls approximately 8,000 students from all regions of Canada.

Another important institution in Fredericton is the large military garrison built in 1825. Although the garrison has not been used to house soldiers and officers since 1869, its stone buildings now contain the York-Sunbury Historical Museum, which is the largest community museum in the province. During the summer, a military band in British uniforms performs the Changing of the Guard ceremony in the garrison's courtyard.

Fredericton's Christ Church Cathedral, built in 1845, is the seat of the Anglican Church in the province. Being chosen as the site of the Anglican cathedral did much to raise Fredericton's status within the Maritime Provinces during the late 1880s. The cathedral is an architectural wonder with magnificent stained glass windows; a miniature copy of London's Big Ben clock is displayed inside.

New Brunswick's government officials have met in the Provincial Legislature since 1880. The extensive library housed in this building exhibits some impressive historical documents, including a 1783 copy of the Domesday Book (which was the world's first census, compiled in England in the year 1027) and 435 hand-colored copperplate engravings of North American birds by the American naturalist John James Audubon (1785–1851), who visited New Brunswick and drew pictures of its birds and wildlife.

Fredericton has a population of 44,000. Many people are employed by the provincial government. Others work at the University of New Brunswick or at St. Thomas University. A small industrial center, consisting of a few lumber mills and clothing manufacturers, is located in the community of Marysville, in the northern part of the city.

*Santiago el Grande*, by the Spanish painter Salvador Dalí, is one of the best-known works in Fredericton's Beaverbrook Art Gallery.

Although it is only the third largest city in the province, Fredericton has earned a reputation as New Brunswick's cultural center; this is largely the result of the generosity of Lord Beaverbrook, a wealthy newspaper publisher who gave considerable sums of money to Fredericton and New Brunswick early in the 20th century. Lord Beaverbrook was born Max Aitken in Ontario in 1879, but he grew up in New Brunswick. He had an eventful career as a journalist, politician, and financial wizard in Canada and England, and he was knighted by the British crown in 1911. After achieving great wealth, he spent money generously in the capital of his former home province. He built the Beaverbrook Art Gallery, which houses an internationally renowned collection of classical and modern paintings, and provided money to build the Playhouse, the home of Theatre New Brunswick. In addition, he contributed both materials and funds to the University of New Brunswick.

## Saint John

Saint John, located on the banks of the Saint John River at the edge of the Bay of Fundy, is Canada's oldest incorporated city and New Brunswick's busiest port and industrial center. It is also the biggest city in the province, with a population of 76,000.

Like Fredericton, Saint John was originally a fur-trading post and a capital of French colonial interests in Acadia at the end of the 17th century. But—like Fredericton—it now has a distinctly British appearance. Since the first permanent British settlers began arriving in the 1760s, Saint John has attracted thousands of immigrants from England, Ireland, and Scotland.

During the 19th century, the city boomed as a shipbuilding center and then as a port for grain bound from the prairies of western Canada to the cities of Europe. But for much of the 20th century, Saint John has been economically stagnant, steadily losing both jobs and people. Yet the city is able to face the 1990s and beyond with a great deal of optimism. Since 1985, urban renovations have brightened many of the city's once gritty and dilapidated neighborhoods, including the waterfront. Saint John acquired both new athletic facilities and national prestige when it hosted the 1985 Canada Summer Games, an important amateur athletic competition. Its economy received a boost during the 1980s when its largest shipbuilding company received a multi-billion-dollar contract to produce military vessels.

## Moncton

Moncton is the unofficial capital for New Brunswick's Acadian population and also, with a population of 55,000, the province's second largest city. It is situated on the southeastern coast near the eastern end of the Bay of Fundy.

Although more than a third of the city's inhabitants speak French as their primary or only language, and although much of its civic and commercial business is carried on in French, Moncton was actually founded by Dutch and German families who immigrated to New Brunswick from Pennsylvania. Later the city became a British shipbuilding center. But as more and more French-speaking settlers were expelled from other parts of Acadia into northeastern New Brunswick, Moncton became known as the Gateway to Acadia. It is the site of the Acadian Université de Moncton, the Acadian newspaper *L'Evangeline*, and many Acadian political and social organizations.

Hub City is another nickname for Moncton. All railway lines into or out of the Maritime Provinces pass through the city, and the Canadian National Railways is the largest employer in Moncton. Businesses serving the railroads have greatly added to Moncton's economic vitality, helping the city hold its own during much of the 20th century.

Edmundston, in the province's northwest corner, is the center of New Brunswick's forest industries. Many French-speaking people from Quebec settled around Edmundston, and although French is the city's main language, most people also speak English.

Partridge Island, in the harbor of Saint John, was once a quarantine station for immigrants. Today it is a placid residential community.

## Other Communities

New Brunswick is dotted with many smaller communities. Edmundston, in the northwest, is surrounded by deep forests and is a center of the logging and papermaking industries. The well-known folk tales about Paul Bunyan, a legendary woodsman of extraordinary strength, originated in the logging camps of Edmundston. To the east are Campbellton, a rustic town that is the starting point for fishing and camping trips into the Restigouche Uplands; Bathurst, the center of the lead and zinc mining industries; and Dalhousie, a year-round port for oceangoing ships and the site of one of the province's largest paper mills.

Chatham and Newcastle, at the mouth of the Miramichi River, are old-time lumbering and shipbuilding towns; today their economies depend in part upon a military air base and training school built by the federal government. Shippegan is a popular beach resort along the north shore and is also the site of the province's new Marine Museum. Caraquet is noted both for its lively fishing and fish-packing industries and as a center of Acadian culture. And in the interior of the province, the Saint John River flows through dozens of small, placid towns very much like the New England communities that lie across the U.S. border.

Tiny farming communities are strung along the fertile length of the Saint John River valley in the same way that small fishing villages dot the coast. The people of New Brunswick face the challenge of preserving their province's traditional ways of life while encouraging economic growth.

# Things to Do and See

• **Beaverbrook Art Gallery,** Fredericton: This world-renowned museum includes works by Turner, Gainesborough, and Dalí as well as by various Canadian painters. Another highlight is a collection of 18th- and 19th-century porcelain.

• **The Playhouse,** Fredericton: Home of Theatre New Brunswick (TNB), the province's only professional theater company, which also tours around the province.

• **Partridge Island,** Saint John: Now a coast guard station, this island is steeped in history. During the colonial era, it was the site of North America's first quarantine station, where immigrants carrying disease were isolated. The province's first lighthouse and steam-powered fog alarm were built on the island, and a military base was located there from 1800 to 1947. A museum displays exhibits from the island's past.

• **King's Landing,** Fredericton: A historical re-creation of the sights and sounds of New Brunswick in the 18th century. Located on 300 acres (121 hectares), it includes 10 houses, a working sawmill, a gristmill, a small theater, a school, a church, a forge, a store, and an inn.

*Opposite:* A climber surveys the scene from the flank of Mt. Carleton, New Brunswick's highest mountain.
*Above:* Kings Landing Historical Village, near Fredericton, is a re-creation of a settlement of the British Loyalists who flocked to New Brunswick from the United States in the late 18th century.

• **Aquarium and Marine Center,** Shippegan: Exhibits depict the marine life, fishing industry, and human settlements of the Gulf of St. Lawrence region.

• **Huntsman Marine Science Center and Aquarium,** St. Andrews: Exhibits showcase marine life, with emphasis on the creatures of the Bay of Fundy.

• **Flowerpot Rocks,** Hopewell Cape: Sculpted by the mighty Fundy tides, these rock formations resemble giant flowerpots and jars rising from a flat, sandy beach.

• **Acadian Historical Village,** Caraquet: Visitors can relive Acadian history at this re-created settlement, which vividly depicts the Acadian way of life from the late 18th century to the early 20th century.

• **Acadian Museum and Art Gallery,** Moncton: One of Canada's most comprehensive collections of Acadian artifacts, art, and documents, located on the campus of the Université de Moncton.

• **Covered Bridge,** Hartland: This is the longest covered bridge in the world—1,282 feet (390 meters). It was built in 1899 to cross the Saint John River.

• **New Brunswick Craft School,** Fredericton: This is Canada's only postsecondary institution dedicated exclusively to teaching arts, crafts, and design; the school has classes for students and workshops for professional artists and craftspeople.

• **Old City Market,** Saint John: This farmer's market is Canada's oldest indoor market. Dozens of family-operated stalls are housed in a large building designed to look like a ship's hull. Delicious local specialties such as lobster, cheese, and New Brunswick maple syrup are readily purchased; cafés and restaurants were added during a recent renovation.

Roosevelt Cottage on Campobello Island in the Bay of Fundy was the summer retreat of American president Franklin D. Roosevelt. It has been maintained as a museum, complete with Roosevelt's books and sketches.

• **New Brunswick Telephone Museum,** Saint John: Visitors can examine various displays of telephone equipment ranging from a model of Alexander Graham Bell's first telephone to the latest in fiber-optic technology.

• **Cherry Brook Zoo,** Saint John: Located in a wooded setting, this zoo has more than 1,000 animals and represents more than 38 different species. African monkeys, lions, and Siberian tigers are among the exotic and endangered species that inhabit this natural setting.

• **Roosevelt Campobello International Park,** Welshpool: Located on one of the Fundy Islands, this former vacation home of Franklin D. Roosevelt, 32nd president of the United States, is now a museum, containing photos, diaries, and other memorabilia. It was the setting for the movie *Sunrise at Campobello.*

An inner tube gives a young man a wild ride on the Saint Croix River.

# Festivals

***Loyalist Days,*** Saint John (mid-July): Designed to commemorate the arrival of Loyalist settlers in 1783, this festival inspires many of the city's residents to don period costumes for the occasion. The festival includes parades, horse racing, and an antique fair.

***International Festival of Baroque Music,*** Lamèque (mid-July): This annual festival on a tiny northeastern island celebrates the music of Scarlatti, Bach, Vivaldi, and other composers of the 15th, 16th, and 17th centuries. Concerts are held in a parish church that has some of the finest acoustics in the country.

***Shediac Lobster Festival,*** Shediac (mid-July): Performers from around the country and the world entertain in this Acadian fishing village to celebrate the bounty of the sea. Lobster-eating contests and parades are highlights.

***Canada's Irish Festival,*** Chatham/Newcastle (late July): The oldest and largest Irish festival in Canada, this event features entertainers from Ireland, Canada, and the United States. The festival includes dancers, pipe bands, Irish games, films, and craft booths.

***Chocolate Fest,*** St. Stephen (early August): Part of the annual St. Stephen–Calais (Maine) International Festival, this chocolate lover's fantasy includes chocolate meals and chocolate-eating contests. It takes place in the hometown of Ganong's Chocolate Factory, where the chocolate bar was invented.

***Festival-by-the-Sea,*** Saint John (mid-August): This annual two-week festival includes plays and musical performances featuring hundreds of outstanding Canadian actors, dancers, and singers.

*Opposite:* Dancers perform at Saint John's Festival-by-the-Sea, a monthlong event that celebrates the arts and features performers from all of the many cultures represented in the population of modern Canada.
*Below:* Whale-watching tours have become popular summer attractions. Many fishing boats have been newly fitted out as whale-watching tour boats.

# Chronology

| | |
|---|---|
| 1534 | Jacques Cartier sails along the coast of New Brunswick. |
| 1604 | The first French settlement is established in Acadia by Samuel de Champlain and Pierre de Guast. |
| 1691 | The French build Fort Nashwaak at the site of present-day Fredericton. |
| 1713 | The Treaty of Utrecht gives much of Acadia to the British. |
| mid-18th century | The Acadians are forcibly expelled by the British, and British settlers begin to arrive. At this time, present-day New Brunswick is part of the large British colony called Nova Scotia. |
| 1784 | New Brunswick becomes a separate colony. |
| 1842 | The dispute over the border between New Brunswick and Maine is settled. |
| 1867 | New Brunswick becomes part of the Dominion of Canada. |
| 1889 | The Canadian Pacific Railway crosses the province. |
| 1960 | Acadian Louis Robichaud is elected premier of the province. His administration carries out social and economic reforms. |
| 1985 | Saint John hosts the Canada Summer Games. |
| 1990 | New Brunswick makes headlines when premier Frank McKenna suggests changes to the controversial Meech Lake Accord, a constitutional amendment that fails to become law. |

# Further Reading

Boudreau, Amy. *Story of the Acadians*. Gretna, LA: Pelican, 1971.

Brownstein, Bill, et al., eds. *Old New Brunswick: A Victorian Portrait*. New York: Oxford University Press, 1978.

Fingard, Judith. *Jack in Port: Sailortowns of Eastern Canada*. Toronto: University of Toronto Press, 1982.

*Fodor's Canada's Maritime Provinces 1990*. New York: McKay, 1989.

Frideres, James. *Canada's Indians: Contemporary Conflicts*. Englewood Cliffs, NJ: Prentice-Hall, 1974.

Haaland, Lynn. *Acadia Seacoast: A Guidebook for Appreciation*. Edited by Louise Mills and Mercy Johnson. Manset, ME: Oceanus, 1984.

Holbrook, Sabra. *Canada's Kids*. New York: Atheneum, 1983.

Law, Kevin. *Canada*. New York: Chelsea House, 1990.

McNaught, Kenneth. *The Penguin History of Canada*. New York: Penguin Books, 1988.

Nowlan, Alden. *An Exchange of Gifts: Poems New and Selected*. Toronto: Irwin, 1985.

———. *Will Ye Let the Mummers In? Stories by Alden Nowlan*. Toronto: Irwin, 1984.

Trueman, Stuart. *An Intimate History of New Brunswick*. Toronto: McClelland and Stewart, 1970.

Wallis, Wilson Dallam. *The Micmac Indians of Eastern Canada*. Minneapolis: University of Minnesota Press, 1955.

Woodcock, George. *The Canadians*. Cambridge: Harvard University Press, 1980.

# Index

## ACKNOWLEDGMENTS

The Bettmann Archive: pp. 16, 19, 21, 27; © T. Clifford Hodgson: cover, pp. 46, 47, 52; Industry, Science, and Technology, Canada: pp. 3, 5, 8, 31, 32, 35, 38, 49, 53; New Brunswick Department of Tourism: pp. 9, 11, 13, 14, 30, 36, 37, 39, 42, 45, 51, 54, 55, 56, 57, 58, 59; The New Brunswick Museum: p. 20; New Brunswick Natural Resources and Energy Communications: p. 34; New Brunswick Provincial Archives: pp. 22, 28; Notman Photographic Archives, McCord Museum of Canadian History: pp. 17, 24; Saint John Visitor and Convention Bureau: p. 41

**Suzanne LeVert** has contributed several volumes to Chelsea House's LET'S DISCOVER CANADA series. She is the author of four previous books for young readers. One of these, *The Sakharov File*, biography of noted Russian physicist Andrei Sakharov, was selected as a Notable Book by the National Council for the Social Studies. Her other books include *AIDS: In Search of a Killer, The Doubleday Book of Famous Americans*, and *New York*. Ms. LeVert also has extensive experience as an editor, first in children's books at Simon & Schuster, then as associate editor at *Trialogue*, the magazine of the Trilateral Commission, and as senior editor at Save the Children, the international relief and development organization. She lives in Cambridge, Massachusetts.

**George Sheppard,** General Editor, is a lecturer on Canadian and American history at McMaster University in Hamilton, Ontario. Dr. Sheppard holds an honors B.A. and an M.A. in history from Laurentian University and earned his Ph.D. in Canadian history at McMaster. He has taught Canadian history at Nipissing University in North Bay. His research specialty is the War of 1812, and he has published articles in *Histoire sociale/Social History, Papers of the Bibliographical Society of Canada*, and *Ontario History*. Dr. Sheppard is a native of Timmins, Ontario.

**Pierre Berton,** Senior Consulting Editor, is the author of 34 books, including *The Mysterious North, Klondike, Great Canadians, The Last Spike, The Great Railway Illustrated, Hollywood's Canada, My Country: The Remarkable Past, The Wild Frontier, The Invasion of Canada, Why We Act Like Canadians, The Klondike Quest*, and *The Arctic Grail*. He has won three Governor General's Awards for creative nonfiction, two National Newspaper Awards, and two ACTRA "Nellies" for broadcasting. He is a Companion of the Order of Canada, a member of the Canadian News Hall of Fame, and holds 12 honorary degrees. Raised in the Yukon, Mr. Berton began his newspaper career in Vancouver. He then became managing editor of *McLean's*, Canada's largest magazine, and subsequently worked for the Canadian Broadcasting Network and the *Toronto Star*. He lives in Kleinburg, Ontario.

COMMUNITY SCHOOL
Discovery Center

St. Louis, Mo.